EVERYBALL

Reflections, anecdotes and observations
from a life in tennis aimed to tool
you up for the game of life!

MICHAEL JAMES

Everyball

First published in 2016 by

Panoma Press Ltd
48 St Vincent Drive, St Albans, Herts, AL1 5SJ, UK
info@panomapress.com
www.panomapress.com

Book design and layout by Neil Coe.

Printed on acid-free paper from managed forests.

ISBN 978-1-784520-86-1

The right of Michael James to be identified as the author of this work has been asserted in accordance with sections 77 and 78 of the Copyright, Designs and Patents Act 1988.

A CIP catalogue record for this book is available from the British Library.

This book is available online and in bookstores.

DEDICATION

I dedicate this book to the wonderful sport of tennis and all those people within it that have offered me so much of themselves, their time, energy and commitment.

CONTENTS

superb team of coaches led by my trusted lieutenant James Morgan, to develop *Everyball Tennis* beyond a philosophy and into our coaching provider and brand, serving not just Halton, but a number of other clubs, schools and outreach centres where we touch upon 2,000-plus customers per week.

The philosophy of *everyball* forms part of what we now call *The Everyball Way* and I hope that you'll find its elements woven into the fabric of the book as the various reflections, anecdotes and observations unfold.

CHAPTER 2

FIVE MORE MINUTES

Coach Bill Wright, or simply Coach as we still call him, was Head Coach for the University of Arizona Wildcats for 19 years between 1986 and 2005. The Wildcats, as opposed to our arch-rivals the Sun Devils of Arizona State up in Tempe, are more famous for their basketball programme than their tennis, but at the time we were a strong Division 1 team and on one or two brief occasions cracked the top 10 in the NCAA Division 1 rankings.

We played in a tough conference which alongside ourselves and Arizona State included UCLA, USC, Stanford and Cal Berkeley. It was an era in which the conference produced some top professional players, especially in doubles. On many occasions we crossed swords with the likes of Jonathan Stark, Jared Palmer, Alex O'Brien, Byron and Wayne Black, Mark Knowles and Daniel Nestor to name a few. We had no superstars, a team of grafters and workers, *'everyballers'* for sure, that managed on a few occasions to upset the big boys.

Coach had a huge influence on my tennis and ignited my growing ambition to become a coach myself. He is without any doubt one of the most positive, enthusiastic people I have ever met. A short, barrel-chested man, he would get up right close to you and his piercing blue eyes would search deep into yours. A little mischief was never far away and his infectious zest for life could lift any mood, having that gift of making everyone feel special.

Most days after practice at that beautiful moment in Arizona when the sun was just about to set and the heat had gone out of the day, Coach would want to hit a few balls himself and would often single me or my doubles partner Thad Langford out for that purpose. He must have been in his late 50s at the time and didn't move too well, but when he was in position, boy could he 'hit 'em heavy' as he loved to say. 'C'mon MJ, just five minutes,' and I would drag my tired limbs back on to court. Five minutes would turn to 10, and then 10 to 20, until I would appeal to him that I had to get home to study. 'Five more,' he'd reply immediately feeding in another ball that would keep me pinned to the baseline. There was no escape.

And again, five minutes would turn to 10, and 10 to 20 until more often than not, we had been out there for a full hour. But you know, I loved every minute of it because Coach would take such delight in the game, such delight in hitting a 'real heavy one'.

I learned an awful lot from Coach having also worked for him for a summer at his camps in Vail, Colorado. There's no doubt he had a great tennis mind, was a fantastic teacher and motivator, but I guess what really stuck with me was some advice he gave me while we drove back to Tucson in the minibus from a tough loss against the Sun Devils. It was this: make sure you love what you do; embrace it and be passionate about it. Coach was a former lawyer in Los Angeles before he went into full-time coaching, and as a result he always urged us if at all possible to earn a living doing what we loved – whatever that might be.

I couldn't mention Coach without also mentioning his assistant coach for several years Tom Hagedorn. Tom went on from Arizona to be Head Men's Coach at the University of San Diego in 1996 and his outstanding career was sadly cut short when he lost an 18-month battle to leukaemia in March 2009. To this day I'll always remember his favourite response whenever you asked Tom how he was. 'Living the dream!' he would say, 'living the dream.' And he was, because he was cut from the same cloth as Coach Wright, doing each day what he loved, working with players in a sport that he was madly passionate about.

In my first couple of seasons at Arizona I was in the travelling squad but most often 'riding the bench' as the Americans were fond of saying. After a match on the road when the rest of the team were in the physio room or heading back to the hotel, Hagi, as he was affectionately known, and I would go out and do battle for a set or two. We played in some crazy places, all across the United States from Hawaii to Miami and there's no doubt that Tom would have signed up to the philosophy of *everyball.* The courageous purpose with which he faced his illness is a lasting testament to that.

Live your dream and always, but always, make time for five more minutes.

CHAPTER 3

CHARACTER

No man can climb out beyond the limitations of
his own character.

**John Morley, British Liberal Statesman,
writer and newspaper editor.**

I'm not sure where I first came across Morley's quote, but
if we act as if it's true, then those of us with a desire to
get better results ought to invest more into developing our
characters.

How do we do that?

A God-inspired man Paul the Apostle wrote that in order
to develop our character we need to learn to persevere,
and to develop perseverance we need to suffer. Hmmm,
doesn't sound like too much fun does it? But perhaps it
can help us make some sense of those times that we all will
spend in the 'wilderness'.

For the tennis player, time in the wilderness might mean

a bad run of results, loss of form or motivation. It might mean being out for months with an injury or being on the receiving end of a controversial selection decision. Whatever your wilderness experience has or is going to be, you can be sure that it will be a period in which your character is developed. In my opinion, character is a key requirement to help you through those tougher moments in competition as well as life, so let's look to welcome those opportunities we have to suffer just a little bit more!

Many of my wilderness experiences have been whilst injured. I remember my third year playing for the University of Arizona Wildcats. As a 21-year-old 'walk-on' to the team, I had just broken into the starting line-up and was really beginning to contribute to the team's success as we climbed the national rankings, when I took a serious tumble in practice (or what in later years was called the Jurgen-dive by my Buckinghamshire Men's team-mates) falling smack-bang on my playing elbow. Over the next days I developed a serious swelling due to leaking fluid from a ruptured bursa sac in the elbow joint. This in turn developed into an ugly abscess that eventually required quite serious surgery, three lengthy operations in fact. I vividly remember lying in that hospital room, morphine drip at the ready for an open wound stuffed full of some absorption material to soak up the poisonous gunk that was eating away at the muscle, and being flatly told by the specialist that I'd never play tennis again. I thought my world was coming to an end.

On leaving hospital I didn't touch a racket for some time and even looking at one was a reminder of what I was missing, but a gentle but persistent voice kept tugging away at me saying, 'Stuff the advice and get your butt back out there!' So I hit the practice wall left-handed whilst spending hours in the jacuzzi of the Tucson Racquet Club strengthening my right arm and elbow against the current of the pool. Six months later I was back out in full training, ready for what was to be my most successful year as a college player. My elbow has never bothered me since although I've got a nice scar to show for it.

Many years later and now well into my coaching career, I developed serious knee problems. Following a second operation on my right knee, the Harley Street specialist gave me the same doom and gloom advice, 'No more tennis Mike.' For months I took his advice to heart, changing my movement and coaching habits to such a degree that I became fearful of a simple squat. This was until I was encouraged to see a local physio who gave my knee a thorough examination and then asked me to drop into a dreaded squat! As I looked at him in horror, I grabbed the nearest chair to help ease myself down. He immediately swatted my hands away from the chair and barked, 'Squat!' So down I went, expecting my knee to explode at any second. I made it of course, and his summary was, 'Don't worry mate, I've seen far worse than this in my rugby players and got them back on track, so this'll be no problem.' True to his word, with the right rehab programme I was back playing and squatting for Great Britain (not literally!) and although I'll never be a marathon runner, my knees are holding up beautifully as I head towards 50!

Even gold is subject to the refiner's fire, so character-forming wilderness experiences like I've just described ought to be treasured! Unconventional, counter-culture thinking of course, but that's what *everyball* is all about

– did you notice those three Cs in the ethos: curiosity, courage and creativity? Curiosity is our antidote against blindly accepting herd wisdom as I almost did. We need courage to turn in the face of it, and we need creativity to find another solution. Hang on to those three Cs, they're important.

And oh, Paul goes on to say that the end product of suffering, perseverance, and character is hope, or in our context as *'everyballers'* an optimistic view of the future and what we can achieve.

CHAPTER 4

BEWARE THE WOODPECKER!

Back in the early noughties the pastor of my local church in Berkhamsted was a Scot called Billy Milton. Billy is one of life's genuine good guys. He married Suzie and me and I consider him to this day one of my greatest mentors and friends. He is a strong leader and a tremendous speaker, armed with hundreds of stories to help illustrate a particular point he might be making.

One such story involved the space shuttle Discovery that was grounded a few years back, not by technical difficulties or lack of government funding or even by adverse weather conditions, but by woodpeckers. Yellow-shafted flicker woodpeckers found the insulating foam on the shuttle's external fuel tank irresistible material for pecking. The foam is critical to the shuttle's performance. Without it ice forms on the tank when it is filled with super-cold fuel, ice that can break free during lift-off and damage the giant spacecraft. The shuttle was grounded until the damage was repaired.

Billy's point was that we probably all have a number of 'woodpeckers' in our lives who are poised to halt our mission if we pay them too much attention. They are the people who seem to have a particular talent for seeing the obstacles to achieving our dreams and are the first to say, 'Why are you doing that?' or 'You can't possibly think that will work,' or 'I wouldn't risk it if I were you.' They are also the people that at the first failure will say, 'I told you so,' or 'There was no way you were going to do it anyway!'

So, beware the woodpecker!

This is especially important when you are in the early phases of an ambitious project, or following through on a dream or a B HAG, which stands for a big, hairy, audacious goal! On returning to Halton Tennis Centre in 2002 at a time when the club was literally on its knees, I clearly remember the vision I communicated to the club members, players and parents: within five years we would become a standard-bearer within British tennis and an example of best practice in the sport, developing an outstanding club with world-class junior players. We would receive visitors from around the country and be on the front cover of a national magazine.

In essence we were reaching for the stars! And boy did the woodpeckers come a peckin'!

It was always on those days when you had just no more to give – all your energy and drive was used up and then... peck, peck, peck! Most often a snipe here and a comment there, but sometimes something more substantial; something that would take you intellectually and emotionally away from the goal, a situation to divert your focus enough that the mission would be placed in jeopardy. It was at these times that my colleague and great friend James would faithfully remind me, 'Mike, don't let the woodpeckers grind you down.' And I would think of Billy, think of the Discovery, laugh, and then refocus my efforts.

Several years down the line we became and still are one of the country's premier High Performance Centres – what is in essence a village club punching several divisions above our weight with the big boys. Three players have competed at Junior Wimbledon, one of them reaching the top 10 in the world. We have welcomed Tennis Scotland and numerous other clubs and organisations to see what we were are doing, and made it on to the front cover of the magazine *British Tennis*.

I'm pretty sure that we've all got a woodpecker somewhere in our lives, and whilst I wouldn't want to give the beautiful bird a bad name, don't let them peck you into submission!

On 16 December 2012, one of my colleagues, Jemima King, sent me a poem by Edgar Guest called *It Couldn't Be Done* that was read out during that year's BBC Sports Personality of the Year Awards which I think sums this chapter up brilliantly.

Somebody said that it couldn't be done,

But he with a chuckle replied,

That 'maybe it couldn't' but he would be one

Who wouldn't say so till he'd tried.

So he buckled right in with the trace of a grin

On his face. If he worried he hid it.

He started to sing as he tackled the thing

That couldn't be done, and he did it.

Somebody scoffed, 'Oh, you'll never do that;

At least no one ever has done it';

But he took off his coat and he took off his hat,

And the first thing we knew he'd begun it.

With a lift of his chin and a bit of a grin,

Without any doubting or quiddit,

He started to sing as he tackled the thing

That couldn't be done, and he did it.

There are thousands to tell you it cannot be done,

There are thousands to prophesy failure;

There are thousands to point out to you, one by one,

The dangers that wait to assail you.

But just buckle in with a bit of a grin,

Just take off your coat and go to it;

Just start to sing as you tackle the thing

That 'cannot be done' and you'll do it.

CHAPTER 5

TAKE A 30,000-FOOT VIEW

Coaching is a passionate business. To be successful I believe you have to put yourself emotionally on the line every day and engage 100% with those you are working with. Anything less just isn't good enough. I'm often asked what I think are the key ingredients to becoming a successful tennis coach. I don't think I'd be far wrong by saying: a transparent love for the game, total enthusiasm, and a burning desire to see people improve.

The consequence of trying to embody these qualities has at times meant getting myself into an emotional fog. By this I mean that I have given some situations far too much weight and personal thinking time to a point where for short periods it dominates my life. To coin an old phrase it becomes very difficult to see the wood from the trees. We are not involved in a business that you can just switch off when you walk through the door at home at the end of the day, and I am certainly not a person who has the ability to compartmentalise in a way that some of my colleagues are able to do.

Through the years at Halton, I came to know a fantastic couple, John and Vicki Walker. It was John, amongst others, who had persuaded me to come back to the club after three years away working for Tennis Scotland and then Hertfordshire LTA. At various times I had coached both John and Vicki, but it was only in his role as chairman of the club that I really got to know John and continue to be mentored by him now. He's a guy for whom you'll always drop whatever you're doing for a five-minute chat because you know you'll more often than not come away with a couple of nuggets.

The job I returned to at the club was an interesting one, in that there wasn't one! I had handed in my notice as County Performance Officer for Hertfordshire LTA to return to a club that was actually weeks away from going bust and getting boarded up. There was one part-time coach, membership was declining rapidly, the facilities were in dire need of a face-lift at the very least and morale was as low as a proverbial snake's belly! What a challenge!

We set about getting the club off its knees with some real visioning and sound planning, but most of all it was about turning the ship around with personal endeavour, passion, and sheer enthusiasm. We had to breathe life into a dying body, and the only way was through force of will and character. The personal investment in time, energy and emotion was huge, and so you can probably imagine how at times we really couldn't see the wood for the trees.

During these times, John had a great way of defusing things and getting us back on track. 'Why don't we take a little look at this from 30,000 feet?' It was an amazing way of simply giving us a little bit of perspective. At ground level, all you see is what's immediately around you. You

As we began the third, the light began to fade and if you've ever spent time in East Africa you'll know that at dusk darkness comes on quickly. The tension was also mounting as we continued to trade games with very little to choose between us, but being the younger brother with nothing to lose and a greater motivation to prove myself, the flow of momentum finally began to run my way.

And then, in the rapidly dying light, the big moment finally arrived: a match point to me, 5-4 in the third set, 40-30, serving to the ad side where I could get a good look at Steve's backhand return. A later chapter talks about playing *everyball* with 'courageous purpose' – doing the right thing, at the right time, at the right place, with conviction. I'm absolutely ashamed to say that I failed miserably in this regard because as I shuffled the balls in my hand ready to deliver my first serve, it was a white ball that finally nestled neatly between my fingers.

There was the briefest moment of hesitation as a thin smile spread across my face, and then I delivered the hardest, most accurate serve that I had ever hit. Impossible for even a hawk-eyed professional to pick up the flight of the ball in such circumstances, it found the edge of the line beyond the reach of my brother's racket that had of course arrived far too late.

Would he have returned it had I used the yellow ball as agreed? I don't know, and I certainly didn't wait to argue the matter or even shake hands, for as the ball rebounded against the fence behind, my mother's cry for supper was heard, and the match was, well, over, and victory was mine.

With the work I now do with **CHILDS** (The Chiltern Institute of Learning, Development and Sport, see curiouscows.uk) we have defined winning as 'identifying, gathering and mobilising all our resources to go as far as we can'.

Little did I know it, but on that murram court built lovingly by Dad for his two boys, I was clearly living out the definition, albeit a little deviously, 40 or so years before its time!

Yes, balls matter – choose 'em carefully!

CHAPTER 8

COURAGEOUS PURPOSE

There's a fair bit of 'tennis talk' and jargon in this chapter, but nothing the non-tennis player shouldn't be able to get their head around. Stick with me for a few minutes and hopefully there's a nice little nugget at the end!

In the book's introduction you will have read the first line of the *everyball ethos*. I use this word interchangeably with *philosophy* as I tend to define an ethos as 'a way of doing something' whilst philosophy is 'a way of thinking'. *Everyball* is a way of both *doing* and *thinking*! Anyway, that aside, it reads:

We commit to fight for everyball, to run down everyball, and to play everyball with courageous purpose.

Fighting for *everyball* refers to the idea that we're going to do everything to get into the best possible position to play our next shot, preparing racket, body and feet in such a way as to be behind the ball, comfortable and balanced with an ideal impact point 'out in front between shoulder and waist high'. Running down *everyball* is more about the heart and the legs, the determination and physicality to never let a ball past you or to bounce twice in front of you – all 'highlight show' stuff embodied by the likes of Rafa Nadal and Serena Williams: heart and legs working to maximum, things we can admire and emulate and for the kids go out and practise every day.

But what does playing every ball with *courageous purpose* mean? We talk of 'purpose' all the time in terms of there being an intention behind every shot – whether to rally, attack or defend, so what's with the 'courageous' bit?

Well, I believe that courage is '*doing the right thing at the right time and in the right place, and doing it with conviction'*.

I'm a big Federer fan but I'll never forget the US Open semi-finals of 2011 against Novak Djokovic. Federer is 5-3 up in the fifth set of an epic encounter serving at 40-15, two match points in hand. In most cases this is as good as game over and the pro-Federer crowd were going nuts. As Fed stepped up to the line for the *coups de grace*, Djoko set himself to respond. Federer swung his first serve out wide to the Djokovic forehand and he lunged out to the ball and simply crunched it for an untouchable winner back down Federer's line. It was such an audacious shot to pull off, filled with so much daring, courage and conviction, you could only but applaud. It changed the course of the match and Djokovic completed a stunning come-back to win and has since pretty much dominated the sport.

Yet Djokovic is also able to play another kind of shot with courageous purpose and this is why I salute him as the greatest example of playing in this *everyball* kind of way. This time it's 15th seed Stanislas Wawrinka serving to stay in the 2013 Australian Open final against No.1 Djokovic at 10-11 in the fifth set. Wawrinka misses his first serve but hits a good second, jamming Novak's forehand. After trading 10 or so hard-hit groundstrokes, Wawrinka gets the upper hand in the point and pummels away with his forehand at a scrambling Djokovic. Ball 14, Djokovic defends a skidding shot off his baseline giving Wawrinka a shorter ball to attack to the No.1's backhand side. With surely his legs screaming in pain and his heart just wanting the point over, every impulse in Djockovic on ball 16 must have been to pull the trigger and go for broke down-the-line, sh-- or bust! Not so, he *chooses to suffer* just a bit more in search of victory and sends the ball back cross-court to stay in the point. Still under pressure on ball 18 he plays a defensive slice backhand to an approaching Wawrinka, which finally sets him up for the backhand angled pass on shot 20 of the point to win the match and the title. What followed was his famous ripping off his shirt and lion's roar. Credit to him – the greatest exponent of playing with courageous purpose the game has ever seen. You can see both these points on YouTube. I often play them to our younger players to bring this aspect of *everyball* to life.

What might be the right thing to do in one situation is the wrong thing in another, and I suppose we're all asked to do the courageous thing on a day-to-day basis, not just on the tennis court.

Right thing, right time, right place, with conviction. Have a courageous day!

CHAPTER 10

KNOWING WHEN TO QUIT

(Although based on a true story, all names in it
are fictional)

At the beginning of my coaching career in my early 20s,
I often struggled teaching adult groups. It was sometimes
difficult to relate to my older clients, I was a little unsure
of myself, and I generally felt more comfortable working
with the up-and-coming juniors where my own game
and role-modelling could do most of the talking. Not at
all surprising as I see this now in some of our younger
coaches on the team, but funny how life moves on as I
absolutely love working with adults now.

During those early days we ran an intermediates section
of the club which was a little like a rusty rackets section
for those who hadn't played for a long time or indeed were
new to tennis. Every Thursday evening between 7pm and
9pm I would have four adults at a time for half-hour drills
sessions, and those two hours became a source of weekly
anxiety for me. And for good reason.

One of our intermediate members was a chap called Greg. Greg was, simply put, a disagreeable man, rightly unpopular with the rest of the membership because of his startling capacity for rudeness. Very rarely would you get a smile out of him and although he could play quite well himself, he was often very condescending towards others and their playing ability and just didn't really make the effort to engage at all. Perhaps every club of any kind has a Greg, but on this particular summer evening, he was on top form.

A week or so earlier, I had warmly welcomed a rather timid but lovely man, Jonathan, into the club. He was mid-40s, married with a couple of kids, and was turning to tennis to keep himself active as he was deskbound most of the week. I had sold the club to him on the fact that it was such a friendly place to be, he'd make loads of friends in no time and it wouldn't be long before he'd bring the family down to join him. Jonathan confessed that he was not overly blessed on the coordination or athletic side, but no matter I said, we'd get him playing in no time.

My 7.30pm group had just finished, which included Greg at his surly, sneering best, looking like he wanted to be anywhere but on my court. As the next group ambled on I noticed that there were only three of them including Jonathan who was gently swishing his old T2000 (made popular by Jimmy Connors 20 years before!), ready for his first session at the club. So to make up a four, I asked if one of Greg's group wanted to stay. I couldn't believe Greg would as I suspected that he'd far sooner go and upset another section of the membership, but to my horror he put up his hand. My heart sank but I didn't have the courage to say anything other than, 'That's great Greg, thanks a lot!'

And so we began with the 'butterfly drill'. A very simple exercise where the coach feeds the ball out of the basket to player A who plays a forehand, recovers to the middle, then moves out to play a backhand, recovers to the middle and then the process is repeated again to make a four-ball 'side-to-side' drill. Player B then steps up while A goes down the other end to pick up a few balls.

Greg, of course, went first, and smugly played all his shots with a smooth accuracy towards the cross-court targets I had placed out on court and began jogging around to pick up balls. Next up is Jenny, not quite as smooth, but responding well to my tips and encouragement. 'Well done Jenny, racket back a little sooner, that's it, low to high with the swing now!' And off Jenny goes to be replaced by Patrick who goes through his paces being nervously watched by Jonathan, racket no longer swishing but held rather tight to his chest as if fearing what it might produce.

Jonathan finally steps up for his maiden butterfly drill just as Greg has dumped his balls in my basket and is returning down the hitter's end. I feed the first ball into Jonathan, and with a rather disjointed swing (big backswing and no follow-through for the tennis aficionados out there) he makes clean contact. So clean in fact that the ball flies well over the back fence into the dense undergrowth behind the court. Hmmm, I think to myself as I notice Greg stop dead in his tracks. 'Close that racket face a little, Jonathan,' I say with a smile, 'don't worry we've got plenty of balls!'

I feed ball two in, this time to Jonathan's backhand as I clench my jaw, squint my eyes and hope for the best. All arms and legs, Jonathan makes another clean contact. Again, so clean that ball two sails high over the fence. No change in facial expression from Jonathan other than a quizzical look at the T2000, but by this time Greg has returned to his position in line and the beginnings of a smirk appear on his face. I maintain my cheery positive outlook, ignoring that two brand new balls are history. 'OK, Jonathan, let's try that forehand again. Remember, close the face at contact.'

The next minute or so seems to happen in super-slow motion. I recall ball three in my left hand, my palms now a little sweaty as I get ready to feed. Greg, Jenny and Patrick are now all waiting in line and there are a few casual onlookers whose attention has now been drawn to the coaching court. I place ball three perfectly to give Jonathan every chance of playing a successful shot but his now familiar wind-up fills me with dread and he's rewarded by a third straight missile clean over the fence. I'm sure I can see the 'Wilson US Open' writing on the ball so still was it in the air as it raced to settle in another bed of nettles.

I steal a quick glance at Greg again, but his back is now turned and he looks as if his shoulders are shaking uncontrollably. I'm at a loss of what to say to Jonathan so I offer him a weak smile.

Now you tell me... do you feed in the final ball? I had a few seconds to deliberate. Don't feed it and you leave Jonathan embarrassed at his failure. Feed it in, and I stand to lose another ball and face the unpredictability of Greg's behaviour. And how would Jonathan cope with four clean home-runs?

Surely not four in a row?

I steel myself and go for it with a final wince at Jonathan's laboured preparation. Then suddenly we're no longer in slow motion and the rest of this hideous experience happens in a flash. Ball four of course flies over the fence, Jonathan's hands go to cover his face, and Greg turns around and says loudly, 'Oh my God he's done it again,' before bending over, hands on knees, in convulsions of laughter. I must admit to muttering quietly under my breath without my lips moving, 'F'ing hell, he's done it again...'

I can't recall how I rescued the situation or if I even did, but that was our 7-9pm intermediates session at its very best.

The life lesson in this one? Know when to quit and hold off feeding that next ball!

You may be interested to know that soon after that Greg left the club and may well be plying his fearful trade elsewhere. Do let me know if you come across him. Some 15 years on, Jonathan and his lovely wife are still with us, enjoying their tennis and have become wonderful contributors to all we do.

CHAPTER 11

PRACTISE WHAT YOU PREACH, COACH!

In 20-plus years in the coaching industry, I've delivered plenty of workshops on the role of the parent in raising children in and around sport. All the basics: avoid giving advice, ask 'Did you enjoy yourself?' as opposed to 'Did you win?' or 'Did you score?', be invisibly visible, let them pack their own racket, don't dissect the performance on the way back in the car, etc., etc.

Last year I took my elder son off to an LTA (Lawn Tennis Association) Grade 4 12&U event. Joel enjoys his tennis but is not a regular member on the local junior circuit, so my chances to see him play and be the role model tennis parent are few and far between.

Still, there we were at Letchworth Tennis Club having arrived early and had a little hit. I tried my best not to give him any advice and failed, 'Remember, get that ball toss up high enough.' He was to play a kid he'd beaten before in a summer camp so he thought he was on for a win, but the kid looked like he'd been working on his game. 'Don't take this for granted, be consistent and he'll miss,' were my parting comments before the match began.

I sat a few courts away at a table, laptop out trying to maintain that facade of 'I'm just here to enjoy watching you play.' Well, it took the entire match to write a short email, although I did have a nice conversation with the club's head pro which took my focus away from the match for a while.

The boys split the first two sets and went into a 10-point champ tiebreak (first to 10 points, win by two). Joel went up 9-7 and on his first match point played a cracking forehand that he (and I from my vantage point several courts away) thought painted the line. Halfway down on to his knees in celebration (yes, possibly a bit dramatic for a first-round grade 4 event) and his opponent called the ball long. Tough call, but all the credit to him though as he dusted himself off ready for another chance to end it all, but it wasn't to be and he lost 11-9.

He managed to hold back the tears until he got into the car, and after a little pep talk, 'It's a tough sport' and all that, he began to feel a bit better. And oh, that match point was well and truly dissected.

So to all you parents out there supporting your kids in all their endeavours, I know what you're going through, folks, and just to give you a little honesty, it's tough to practise what you preach! Stay calm, feign indifference, act the adult... I think it's easier to watch your kids rather than mine. I'll stick to doing just that!

Joel spent some time at Luton Football Club's Centre of Excellence and I pinched a very simple acronym from them. The descriptions of each word I developed out myself although heavily influenced by the likes of Dr Carol Dweck (*Mindset*) and Daniel Coyle (*The Talent Code*), two books that I have drawn deeply from over the past few years. I hope it can be of some help.

At *Everyball Tennis* the parental role in developing our young athletes is a challenging and vital one, and we use the P.A.R.E.N.T.S. acronym to define it:

Praising
Accepting
Recognising
Encouraging
Nurturing
Teaching
Supporting

Praising We praise for doing rather than being. We praise 'best effort' over outcome.

Accepting We accept that it is our children's journey not ours, and understand that parents living their own dreams, hopes and aspirations through their children run the risk of increasing pressure on them which can lead to adverse effects on emotional control, motivation and well-being, impacting the ability of the athlete to perform at their best.

Recognising We recognise that there is nothing fixed about our children. Their potential is defined entirely by their ability to develop skills, with effort, over time. In this, learning behaviours are valued over comparative behaviours, where improving is better than proving. (Dr

Carol Dweck, *Mindset)*

We recognise what is true and positive about our children's performances and behaviours.

Encouraging We 'give courage' and strengthen their determination. We encourage through dos rather than don'ts.

Nurturing We nurture by wilfully exposing our children, within the safe environment of sport, to life. We nurture a sense of ownership and responsibility in them for their own actions and behaviours, promoting a 'personal responsibility in developing excellence' (P.R.I.D.E).

Teaching We teach through our own behaviours and actions – they speak more powerfully than words. Teaching is not always 'telling' and we might consider that the quality of our communication can only be measured by the response we get. Teaching might also mean allowing them to make their own mistakes and learn from the consequences.

Supporting We support with unconditional love and by being **visibly invisible** – allowing our children the space to express themselves and develop other relationships (be that with peers, coaches, other adults) outside of parental reach, eye contact, or influence.

All the very best of luck.

CHAPTER 12

I KNOW

Anyone in the coaching, teaching, mentoring or even, dare I say after the last chapter, the parenting business, will have come across the 'I know-er'.

I coached a classic 'I know-er' for many years, Rhonda (not her real name). What's an 'I know-er'? Well, let me play this out for you.

Me (when Rhonda's missed five forehands on the trot): 'Hey Rhonda, get that contact point a little further out in front of you, OK?'

Rhonda: 'Yep, *I know*.'

Me (when working on Rhonda's service action): 'Think that ball toss is a little bit too far back Rhonda, that's why the ball's going long every time.'

Rhonda: 'Yep, *I know*.'

Me: 'Rhonda, that racket preparation is a little bit late again (it was always late, every time; read the next chapter on absolutes!).

Rhonda (with some variation): 'Ah, yep, thanks, *I know*.'

It would infuriate me. If you *know*, why don't you do something about it!? Make a change, do something, do anything, but for goodness' sake, STOP SAYING 'I KNOW'!!

Not so long ago I was re-reading WT Gallwey's book *The Inner Game of Tennis (*a fantastic little 'life learning' book whether you're a tennis fan or not. He went on of course to write *The Inner Game of Golf, The Inner Game of Music,* and even *The Inner Game of Work).*

A particular observation he makes on learning jumped out at me: *By the word learning, I do not mean the collection of information but the realisation of something which actually changes your behaviour.*

Yes, exactly Rhonda, it's not just about knowing, but making change!

With greater reflection however, I began to recognise my ineffectiveness in helping Rhonda make those changes. Could I have explored further ways of creating lasting change in Rhonda's game rather than a reliance on the simple instructions I expected her to obey? Of course! I could have illustrated the point better, changed my communication style using more visual tools, created more curiosity in her, or improved her kinaesthetic awareness in more creative ways.

Fundamentally I believe that as coaches we can lay far too much at our students' feet in terms of our expectations of them simply to learn. I hear so often, 'They just won't change' or 'I can only lead them to water, but they've gotta drink!' One of NLP's (Neuro Linguistic Programming) belief frames is 'the meaning of communication is the response we get'. How very true.

Our promise to our customers at *Everyball Tennis* is to 'educate, motivate, and inspire through the power of sport to help you become the best you can be.' The words educate, motivate and inspire are carefully chosen, and in particular relation to this chapter is motivate, meaning to cause to take action.

If we are motivational coaches, teachers, mentors and parents we 'cause' our learners to take action. That action most often leads to change.

Is knowing stuff (information) important to learning? Yes it is, because it's part of the trilogy of inform, form, and transform. But at the heart of learning is the forming of new behaviours that leads to transformational change.

CHAPTER 13

ABSOLUTES AND A FEW OTHER WORDS BESIDES

How are you for 'absolutes'? Once your antennae are up you'll hear them all the time. Take my two sons. I'll often hear them say, 'Daddy, you *always* say that...' or 'Daddy, you *never* let me...' My wife will often say, 'Mike, you *never* take out the bins!' My response to them, and certainly risking marital warfare where Suzie is concerned is, 'always?', 'never?'. 'C'mon, sometimes I do!' Brave? Foolish? Yes, though there is an important message here.

I continue to spend some time working with Britain's 20-year-old fourth ranked tennis player Katy Dunne (according to rankings as of November 2015). I began coaching Katy when she was 11 years old, and during her long association with us at Halton and *Everyball Tennis* she cracked the world's top 10 in the junior rankings and is well on her way to a successful professional career. A fantastic kid, great sense of humour, character in spades, with a fair old temper and a whole load of grit and guts.

In her younger teens I spent a lot of time on the road with Katy, in Europe and extensively around Great Britain. She got to the second round of Les Petits As, the unofficial 14&U World Championships held in Tarbes, France before falling ill and having to withdraw, and won the 16&U National Championships during a particularly fruitful time for her. But it was never without its ups and downs, and I remember a period where Katy had lost four or five matches on the bounce, each time losing from a winning position in the third set.

On one occasion Katy came storming off court, tears of anger rolling down her face, threatening to give up and protesting how much she hated tennis! 'I always lose when I'm serving for it in the third. Always!' she blurted out. 'Always?' I asked gently. 'Yes, always!' she fired back and stomped off to cool down and shower.

About 45 minutes later I was quietly having a coffee whilst gathering her match stats together and Katy came over to join me, sufficiently recovered, for our normal post-match briefing. 'Well, not *always,*' she somewhat sheepishly opened up. 'Oh,' I said, 'so tell me about the last time you won from 5-3 up.' And she did, remembering it quite clearly as it was only a couple of months beforehand. And of course, the solution was there. With a little questioning, she described how she managed to serve out the match, 'I just stayed focused on where I wanted to serve and what I wanted to do in the point, and managed to keep that focus when the point actually began. The last few matches, my thoughts between points have been drifting too much to the finish line, what it would mean to my ranking if I win and all that kinda stuff.'

Often the difference is in how big we see the problem and how small we see the solution, or how big we see the solution and how small the problem. And often, the solution is right there in front of us; a great example of identifying, gathering and mobilising our resources to go as far as we can!

Words do matter. For example, take these few little words that carry big meaning:

Don't, *Try* and *But*, *Can't* and Y*et*.

Don't think of the blue tree!!! Chances are you've got an image of a blue tree in your head, right?

'*Don't* swing so much.'

'*Don't* set those feet too early.'

'*Don't* just hoof it' (from my son's opposing football manager this morning).

Thing is, we don't hear the *don't*. All we hear is the other bit: 'swing, set early, hoof it!' so where possible it's so important to prescribe the remedy not the post-mortem. It just requires a little more thought:

'Shorten that swing, block more.'

'Keep those feet moving a little longer.'

'Pass the ball out.'

I'm sure you can think of plenty more examples.

How about 'try'? It even merited a chapter in Bear Grylls' *A Survival Guide for Life.*

Bear writes: *Maybe it's just me, but I don't like the word try* (we'll give him the word *don't* there, shall we?). ***Trying*** *to do something just sounds like you're not really making that much effort – and the result is almost inevitable. Somewhere in our brains the word try gets associated with phrases like: 'He tried his best' and 'Try again' or 'I'll try to make it'. It's almost as if* ***trying*** *to do something means you're setting yourself up to fall short of your goal. So I swap the word try for the better version:* ***endeavour***.

But is an interesting one. Compare these two pieces of feedback:

'Holly, that was a good match out there today *but* next time more spin on that second serve, OK?'

OR:

'Holly, that was a good match out there today *and* next time more spin on that second serve, OK?'

It might seem innocuous enough but *but* negates the whole first part of the sentence doesn't it? Where possible, *don't* use *but*, and *try* to use *and!* No, let's do that again: whenever you can, endeavour to use *and*.

Eliminate those two little words from your everyday conversations and see how that influences mindset and behaviour, both in yourself and others.

You may also want to consider *can't* and *yet*. It's so common to hear, 'I can't do it/understand it/get it' etc. as a response to the introduction of a new idea, skill or competency. And in many cases, that's probably quite true, though just adding a *yet* at the end of the sentence changes everything.

'I can't do this, *yet*' or even better, 'I'm struggling hard with this and not quite there *yet*.' One of our key beliefs at *Everyball Tennis* is 'becoming is better than being' and just by consistently challenging our students to reframe their language makes a significant difference to their mindset and also the learning culture within the programme.

And finally, just a thought on *good*. I mentioned Holly above. She's great friends with Katy, a couple of years younger with an absolutely unquenchable love for tennis and competition. A really wonderful kid to work with. Having broken into the world top 200 juniors and played at Junior Wimbledon in 2014 and 2015, you can imagine Holly's got some 'game'. In fact, she's got a fearsome forehand, and for much of our time together as player and coach, it's really been off limits in terms of development work. 'Let's not touch the forehand,' she'd say, 'it's good.'

For a while I had no comeback, until earlier this year I was fortunate enough to spend a day with Louis Cayer, the great doubles specialist working for the Lawn Tennis Association. One of his favourite sayings that he credits to Jim Collins and his book *Good to Great* is *'good is the enemy of great'*. I thought of Holly immediately and couldn't wait to use it with her. Sure enough, a couple of weeks later the subject of her forehand came up again, and again the same closed doors until I half-whispered to her, 'Hmmmm, do you think good could be the enemy of great?' It's been open season on her forehand ever since and what was good internationally is now becoming great internationally.

Choose your words carefully, especially the little ones!

The Everyball journey begins on the murram courts of Nairobi at the Kenya Open 10&U Doubles in 1978.

The fight for everyball continues on the hard courts of Tucson, Arizona in 1985

Everyballers Katy Dunne and Holly Hutchinson play at Junior Wimbledon. Katy pictured in 2011 and Holly in 2015. Photos taken by Chris Duffin.

The home of Everyball Tennis. The beautiful Rothschild clubhouse at Halton UK was originally a cricket pavilion in the early 1900s, with the pitch being replaced with grass courts for use by the officers of RAF Halton. Photo taken by Chris Duffin.

CHAPTER 14

THE QUALITY OF OUR MOTIVATION MATTERS

Yep, the quality of our motivation matters – it matters a great deal.

You'll know that there are two basic types of motivation: intrinsic and extrinsic.

Extrinsic motivation is externally generated, normally via a 'carrot and stick' approach or the external reward for one's efforts, such as finances, praise, recognition and fame being examples. The thinking often goes, 'If you want people to perform better, you reward them.' Interestingly, and the subject of a great TED talk by Dan Pink titled 'The Puzzle of Motivation' (filmed in 2009 at TEDGlobal 2009) Dan suggests that 'rewards narrow the focus and solutions, which often are found in the periphery, are missed. Higher rewards in fact are shown to negatively impact performance.'

Intrinsic motivation, on the other hand, is generated more from within and has a deeper, more powerful impact on performance. Pink tells us there are three key building blocks to internal motivation and these can be remembered as AMP. He defines them as:

Autonomy – The urge to direct our own lives, make our own decisions, have a hand in shaping our own destiny.

Mastery – To get better and better at something that matters.

Purpose – The yearning to do what we do in the service of something larger than ourselves, be that contributing to the mission behind one's own family, club, team, or organisation.

In August this year Suzie and I took the boys up to see a Chelsea match, my elder son Joel being a huge fan. Yes, his resolve is being firmly tested now as their 2015 campaign has started miserably! Anyway, it was a lovely day and we took the train up early for a walk along the South Bank to take in the sights. As we neared St. Paul's Cathedral on the opposite side of the river, we came across a skate-park full of skateboarders hard at it. I had never really given 'boarding' much of a look-in, either as a kid or now as a parent; it's a whole culture in itself with its own peculiarities of language and dress code – a bit like tennis I suppose, that you've got to break into.

It was as good a place as any to stop for a sandwich and we just sat there and watched the skateboarders and what struck me was their high level of intrinsic motivation. Their time was purely spent mastering skills, for no other reason than to master something that mattered to them. There was no event, no competition and in many senses you could just call it play. But it was more than that as well.

There was a communal feel about their work, they were helping each other, making a suggestion here or there, and celebrating when somebody nailed a move. Many sat around for periods just chatting, and then for whatever reason, went back to it. They showed autonomy in terms of when to practise, how to practise, and for how long and there was a clear yearning to be part of and contribute to a culture that was larger than themselves. After all, how is a new trick invented and how does it then get disseminated through the skateboarding world? A great example of AMP at work.

It reminded me a little of Roger Federer's new game invention in 2015, the SABR or 'surprise attack by Roger', where he rushes at an opponent's second serve, takes it ridiculously early on the half-volley and smothers the net. It's proved to be incredibly effective and part of Federer's amazing ability for re-birth. According to most reports, the SABR came about through Roger messing around in practice and his coach Stefan Edberg saying to him, 'You should try that in a match!' Again, high intrinsic motivation at work. Federer has a fascination in mastering something that matters deeply to him.

My father knew Bunny Austin quite well having worked with him for a period just after the Second World War. Bunny, as you'll know, was for 74 years the last Briton to reach the men's Wimbledon final until Andy Murray won that amazing match against Novak Djokovic in 2012. He was also finalist at the French Open in 1937 and alongside Fred Perry was part of the victorious Davis Cup team that won the event three consecutive times between 1933 and 1935. For much of his post-tennis life Bunny lived at odds with the British tennis hierarchy and was only re-elected back to the All England Club in 1984. He stayed close to tennis however during these years and was particularly interested in the decline of the game, blaming a welfare state that had emerged.

I have often pondered on this welfare state, and believe that if it exists or existed, it only did so out of the best of intentions, that of providing our junior players with the best facilities, opportunities and resources to develop their games to compete with the very best in the world. But I must admit to falling into this trap in the role of a 'performance director'. We formally provide weekly programmes for our players consisting of individual lessons, squads, strength and conditioning support, and mental skills sessions. Everything is timetabled and overseen by experts. This is all right and good, though there is one thing missing. Kids now rarely pick up the phone to call a mate (or should I say 'message a friend'?) to play a few sets or have a hit. They rarely take a basket out on to court and practise serves on their own. They rarely take themselves out for a run or workout. The provision of activity has taken away something of the AMP in intrinsic.

As well as this, nearly every match a junior now plays in this country has some sort of 'outcome' implication, be that a rating or a ranking. What happened to just playing for playing's sake, playing to master something deeply important to you? I remember clearly the first time I hit a backhand topspin lob. It was out playing one of our several hundred practice sets that we must have played over the years with my great friend in high school called Roger Rogoff, now a Judge in Seattle, Washington. Court 7 at the Tucson Racquet Club. Rog and I had been watching a little Wimbledon upstairs in the bar before hitting the courts and had just witnessed Boris Becker whip up a topspin lob over Edberg in one of their Wimbledon finals.

Out we were then in the Tucson heat battling away and Rog comes in with a fierce cross-court approach. I had a predominantly slice backhand and even up to the age of 16 or 17 rarely came 'over it' so when faced with such situations I would normally chisel the ball down low to the net-rusher, or poke up a defensive lob. But this time, Becker's image was still at the forefront of my brain, ready for retrieval, and suddenly there it was, my first perfect backhand topspin lob! Would I have risked it if there was something more on the line other than two mates looking to master a sport they so dearly loved?

This is why club social tennis is so valuable. I love seeing kids out there playing with our adults at Halton. They're facing things they don't see too often, funky styles and spins which can be very difficult to cope with. Times like these give youngsters the freedom to risk, to play, to invent and problem solve.

Young players who have a growing sense of ownership and responsibility over their tennis and have that mastery driver – the desire to get better and better at something that matters – tend to stay in the game longer and therefore give themselves the best chance of success, leading ultimately to some extrinsic rewards as well! Players whose world evolves around the external drivers of rating, ranking, finance and material gain will often find careers cut short.

One of our core beliefs defined in *The Everyball Way* is summed up by the acronym P.R.I.D.E. **P**ersonal **R**esponsibility **i**n **D**eveloping **E**xcellence. This means taking initiative outside of the recognised coaching environment to improve as well as developing the 'ability to respond' which comes from the nurturing of self-reliant athletes.

As coaches of course, we can't lay all of this at our players' feet and expect them to be suddenly intrinsically motivated. Although appropriate at times, it's easy, and in my opinion often lazy coaching, to extrinsically motivate players. The carrot and stick works for brief periods, that's for sure, motivation by fear being an example, but you don't have to work too hard or be that creative to do that. To coach in a way that encourages self-direction, self-regulation, autonomy, and a way that inspires a sense of mastery and purpose – now that's coaching!

CHAPTER 15

EMOTIONAL LAZINESS AND THE FOUR Rs

Seth Godin, author of the book *Tribes,* writes a fantastic daily blog that I subscribe to.

Godin wrote this in a blog some time back:

I think laziness has changed. It used to be about avoiding physical labor. The lazy person could nap or have a cup of tea while others got hot and sweaty and exhausted. Part of the reason society frowns on the lazy is that this behavior means more work for the rest of us. When it came time to carry the canoe over the portage, I was always hard to find. The effort and the pain gave me two good reasons to be lazy. But the new laziness has nothing to do with physical labor and everything to do with fear. If you're not going to make those sales calls or invent that innovation or push that insight, you're not avoiding it because you need physical rest. You're hiding out because you're afraid of expending emotional labor. This is great news, because it's much easier to become brave about extending yourself than it is to become strong enough to haul an eighty pound canoe.

This brings me, in a roundabout way, to the four Rs within *The Everyball Way*. You'll remember that the last line of the *everyball* philosophy reads:

We know that every ball extends beyond our sport as we learn the fundamental life skills that enable us to thrive in an ever-changing world.

Well, those life skills which we seek to develop within all our training programmes are:

Respect – ourselves and our games, each other and our opponents, the rules and officials.

Resilience – to bounce back from disappointment ready to go again with very best effort.

Responsibility – or the 'ability to respond' to the challenges *everyball* and the sport present by an ever-increasing sense of autonomy and ownership.

Reflection – what went well? Even better if…?

You see, executing the four Rs with any degree of consistency and success requires emotional energy and takes emotional 'work' if you like.

In tennis we happen to be living in perhaps an unparalleled era of sportsmanship and respect, certainly on the men's side with Federer, Nadal, Djokovic and Murray leading the way. Federer especially in my view has such a concern for the current and future state of the game, and his respect for it is enormous. How else would he at almost 35 years old still be hotly pursuing Grand Slam titles as well as treating every tournament victory as if it were his first? His joy in just playing is immense and a great example of a highly intrinsically motivated player, as I mentioned in the previous chapter.

Rafa Nadal also is a wonderful example to us and perhaps the ultimate embodiment of the *everyball* philosophy when it comes to fighting for and running down *everyball*. Humility, and therefore by definition respect, is one of the great pillars of his philosophy as well as viewing it as a weapon. He draws reference to this in his book *Rafa*:

Understanding the importance of humility is to understand the importance of being in a state of maximum concentration at the crucial stages of a game, knowing that you are not going to go out and win on God-given talent alone.

Respect requires emotional energy and work at any level.

Resilience is perhaps the BIG word in sport right now and rightly so. What is it? Alistair Higham, a British coach and world expert on momentum, defines it in terms of how *quickly* a player can recover from set-back and *how many times* (in a match for example, but over longer periods as well) they can do so.

Nadal goes on to say: *That is not to say that I am not afraid, that I don't have my doubts as to how things will go at the start of each year. I do – precisely because I know that there is so little difference between one player and another. But I do think I have a capacity to accept difficulties and overcome them that is superior to many of my rivals.*

Accept difficulties and overcome them.

Resilience requires emotional energy and work.

Responsibility has long been one of my favourite words.

Broken down it's 'the ability to respond', and is a key ingredient to developing greater resilience and mental toughness. The ability to respond is linked so closely with an individual's increasing sense of autonomy and ownership over their improvement and indeed their lives. As young players become the captain of their own ship by taking more decisions for themselves, setting their own goals, packing their own bags, entering their own tournaments, reflecting on each practice session or match and so on, they build up a significant cause for which they will fight. When all is handed on a plate and done for them, the cause becomes less and so does the fight.

Responsibility requires emotional energy and work.

Daniel Coyle wrote a fabulous book called *The Talent Code* that I draw upon again and again.

In his discussion around talent and how it's developed he talks a lot about deep practice: *Deep practice feels a bit like exploring a dark and unfamiliar room. You start slowly, you bump into furniture, stop, think, and start again. Slowly, and a little painfully, you explore the space over and over, attending to errors, extending your reach into the room a bit farther each time, building a mental map until you can move through it quickly and intuitively.*

One of the key phrases in this quote is *attending to errors* and that's where our fourth R comes in: reflection. The ability to self-reflect, look back on an error, a poor performance, unhelpful attitudes or behaviours, and figure out what to do differently next time is fundamental to any sort of success. I'm always interested in how our players react to mistakes. Are they fascinated by them, see them as feedback to improve and therefore attend closely to them, or are they disgusted with them and want nothing at all to do with them? The answer largely determines how far we go towards becoming the very best we can be!

Here's Katy (from Chapter 13) reflecting via text message whilst on tour in Australia this autumn: *Felt like a cloud's been over me and getting really irritated about things that I wouldn't normally have an issue with! Maybe something to do with putting a bit of extra pressure on myself and feeling like the last couple of weeks I've had missed opportunities. Didn't have a good practice yesterday and was thinking pretty negative until I fell asleep. So today was pretty tough, my chimp was out a lot and I struggled to keep him in check. The first (set) she (her opponent) came out firing combined with me not really being on it so lost the set quickly 6-1. Second set I managed to start to focus on some of the right stuff and made it a much closer set of 6-4 that took an hour. I'm glad I went down with some sort of fight.*

Thanks Katy for a great example of self-awareness and reflection. And guess what?

Reflection takes emotional energy and work.

Living out the four Rs? Now that's bravely extending yourself.

C H A P T E R   1 6

YOU REAP WHAT YOU SOW

Watching Andy Murray play fascinates me. His game style is unique to the tour at the moment. Call him a 'mucker', a 'disruptor' or even a 'sniper', there's no doubting the battling, pugilistic mindset he brings to the court. For this reason, I love watching him play perhaps because I fancy myself as a bit of a disruptor (on court at least!) as well.

Andrew Castle was commentating on the GB v USA Davis Cup match in San Diego in 2014 and said during the James Ward versus Sam Querry match, 'You can play better than your opponent or you can make your opponent play worse than you.' It was an interesting comment that I wanted to explore a little more.

What does it mean for you? I often hear from players having lost a match, 'Oh, he/she just made loads of balls. All the tennis came from me. I just missed the final shot in the point.' This may or may not be true given each individual situation, but the message is, 'I'm really much better than my opponent even though I've just come off court losing 6-2, 6-2.' That's missing A LOT of final shots in the point. Fact is the match has been lost and you've been beaten by a player who has made you play worse than them!

Making balls, *everyball* for that matter, consistently asks questions of your opponent and increases the pressure on them as the match wears on. It's an accrual of marginal gains. So often, Murray 'sows' early on in matches by chasing and hustling balls down, sending strong signals to his opponent that hitting past him is going to be tough. He then 'reaps' later on in matches when the pressure mounts and the opponent goes for just that little too much. Novak Djokovic is of course master of this as well.

Murray's influence on his team-mates is notable and I believe in this area particularly. During that tie with the US, Britain's Davis Cup stalwart James Ward was involved in a titanic five-setter with Sam Querry that eventually gave Britain a 2-0 lead after Murray had beaten Donald Young in the first singles.

Sam Querry was serving huge, and backing this up with his ferociously hit forehand looked the more likely winner after taking the third set 6-3. But Ward had been grimly hanging in since the outset, and as he made return after return, ball after ball, the tide began to turn his way as the pressure began to mount in the fourth set. As a re-Ward (sorry, couldn't resist) for his cumulative efforts, Querry began to over-press and misfire in the fifth and Ward ran away with it 6-1. It was a great example of reaping later on in a match what you sowed in the early stages.

Here's another example of reaping what you sow. All students of our great game will be familiar with Brad Gilbert's book *Winning Ugly*. In it he says:

Fortunately for me, tennis matches aren't played on paper. They're played on tennis courts. And because they are I've been able to beat those players and others to the tune of £5,000,000. By 1991 I was eighth on the all-time prize money list. When you add in the endorsements and exhibitions that resulted from those victories my total income from tennis by 1993 is close to £8,000,000. Winning ugly? All the way to the bank.

It happened because I've used whatever talent and skills I do have in a calculated way that maximises their potential; that gives me my best chance to win. It's why I've been able to beat players who are supposedly 'better' than me. You can do the same. Make the most of what you've got. Play better tennis without better strokes.

Gilbert was a great example of reaping what he sowed. He was a superb student of the game and honed his ability to scout, pin-point and go after his opponent's weaknesses. Much of his sowing took place before the match, in his preparation and ultimate readiness to compete. He understood how to make the environment, the situation and his more limited game work for him against those stronger players:

I saw that Stefan Edberg generally preferred to go cross-court on his forehand volley. I wrote down that his one-handed backhand was one of the best in the business (Lendl's was the other). But I also noted that his forehand was not a weapon – extremely weak for a top player. His grip was bad and the whole stroke was not as impressive as everything else in his arsenal. Believe me; I made a note of that because there was very little I could write down about him that was negative.

The fact he reaped financially was a bi-product of all the sowing he did in his match preparation which allowed him to compete against the very best. In this way, Gilbert was a true player of the game as opposed to just a great hitter of the ball.

Where else do we reap what we sow? On the practice court for sure. Patience and persistence over time, staying the course, delaying gratification over some miracle cure or quick fix. In the coaching world we call them 'shoppers', players who bounce from academy to academy in search of the perfect programme that will deliver success for them. Never works that way and success only becomes possible when preparation meets opportunity, with no guarantees.

CHAPTER 17

PUTTING YOURSELF ON THE LINE

Have you ever heard of the meanderthal? Someone who meanders aimlessly about with no clear direction, no goals, unprepared to risk and put themselves on the line?

Reminds me of the quote by Theodore Roosevelt:

It is not the critic who counts; not the man who points out how the strong man stumbles or where the doer of deeds could have done better. The credit belongs to the man who is actually in the arena, whose face is marred by dust and sweat and blood, who strives valiantly... who, at the best, knows, in the end, the triumph of high achievement, and who, at the worst, if he fails, at least he fails while daring greatly, so that his place shall never be with those cold souls who knew neither victory nor defeat.

Tennis is a brutal sport with an ingenious scoring system. You can win more points than your opponent yet still lose the match. Momentum can turn at the drop of a hat and the only point you cannot afford to lose is the last. It's you and only you, no team-mates to call upon, hide behind or drag you through, with of course the exception of events such as the Davis and Fed Cup. You can't run down the clock, you've got to break the finishing tape. Imagine going up 4-0 in the first half of the football match but the scoreboard is reset for the second half, which if you lose by any score, you'll play a third and deciding half. That would add a new dimension to BBC's *Match of the Day*!

Fundamentally, there's nowhere to hide in tennis. The gladiatorial nature of the sport demands that if you want to succeed you put yourself on the line, again and again.

Nowhere for me was this more evident than at Junior Wimbledon 2014. Holly Hutchinson, briefly mentioned in Chapter 13, had just been offered a wildcard into 'qualies' on the back of some excellent performances during that summer. She was ranked just outside the top 300 in the world on the ITF junior circuit, but on her favourite grass courts at Roehampton, she had a wonderful opportunity to push for a spot in the main draw on the hallowed turf of Wimbledon.

The No. 8 seed from France, Tessah Andrianjafitrimo, was Holly's first-round opponent. A tight match that ebbed and flowed all the way saw Holly come out on top 7-5, 7-6, a significant scalp against a very solid player. So then it came down to a straight shoot-out for qualification against Denmark's Emilie Francati, the blonde, six-foot-plus 13th seed. Holly edged the first set 7-6 playing some great tennis, but in the second Emilie began to find her game, delivering knock-out blows with her massive serve and she levelled the match taking the set 6-4. One set it was then to decide who goes home and who takes the short trip to SW19!

Emilie looked strong at 2-1 up but a run of fabulous hitting from Holly and a few courageous forays to the net saw her take and then maintain a lead, and before too long she was serving out the set and match 7-6, 4-6, 6-3. She was through.

The Junior Championships at Wimbledon are held during the second week of the senior event with the first round split over the first Saturday and the second Monday. Luckily Holly was scheduled for the Monday, so she had a day or so of rest and preparation time. It was needed. The effort and excitement of qualification had taken its toll and it was great for Holly to be able to take stock, refuel and refocus her energy to the task ahead, a first-round main-draw match against the world No. 64 Seone Mendez, an athletic and combative Australian training in Spain. These couple of days had also given Holly the chance to get familiar with Wimbledon itself, the crowds on Saturday and some quiet practice at Aorangi (the Wimbledon practice courts) on Sunday, just a couple of courts down from Maria Sharapova, one of Holly's great role models at the time! A first-time match on the Saturday is always tough when you don't know the routine, so everything was set up in Holly's favour to go out and put in a real performance.

Monday arrived and I knew Holly was ready. A self-proclaimed 'show pony' Holly couldn't wait to set foot on to Court No. 3 which was overlooked by Centre Court, its periodic Colosseum-like roar of the crowd adding to the mood as Holly and her opponent arrived on court. Holly would have represented a difficult draw for the young Australian. A qualifier, whatever the ranking, can often be dangerous. With a couple of big wins under her belt, Holly was seeing the ball huge and had an air of confidence about her that would have unsettled all but the very top seeds in the draw.

I love those first few balls hit in the warm-up at Wimbledon. A sense that the moment has arrived and anticipation of things to come. The murmuring of the crowd as they flock in to see the next Brit in action, the concentration on the players' faces as they find their feet on the beautifully manicured lawns, the all-white clothing rule in beautiful contrast to the green surrounds, but matching the perfectly chalked lines. And Holly was middle-ing everything, a great sign.

Finally, the call of 'time' from the umpire and both the girls returned to their court-side chairs. A last swig of water, a quick look towards their 'camps' and a purposeful walk back to the baseline and the call of 'play' to start the match.

Holly starts like a train, serving accurately and consistently to the corners and taking control of the rallies with her forehand. Seone is moving well and in patches shows what she's capable of, but Holly is too strong and takes the first set 6-3.

As described in an earlier chapter, it can so often be the case that on winning the first set your opponent redoubles their effort, while perhaps you drop your level just a little and the difference can be immediately reflected on the scoreboard. This appeared to be the case and the balance of the match swung heavily in the Australian's favour as she levelled the match with a 6-2 set.

A set all and it would have been easy to think that Holly's moment had come and gone, but one look at her face as she got out of her chair told me otherwise. She was still in this and my sense was that we were in for a cracking third set. We were not to be disappointed. If putting herself and her game on the line was the requirement of the day, Holly stepped up big-time. She plays a 'live by the sword, die by the sword' brand of tennis, and taking anything remotely short and dispatching it with total conviction, Holly broke serve to take a 3-1 lead in the final set. At this stage there looked to be only one winner and as Holly held serve a couple of games later for a 5-3 lead, thoughts of her getting through crossed my mind. I stole a glance or two at Holly's parents, both calm and supportive, no doubt as I was suppressing the tension and all the 'what ifs' that come with the situation Holly was now in.

Who will she play next round? Will she get some national press? Won't this be great for the programme and really put us on the map? Where will it take Holly's ranking?

Come on Holly, one point at a time kiddo... stick to the process!

And boy, did she ever. Two winning returns brings it to two match points and the feeling of inevitable victory is now palpable. Seone steps up 15-40, 3-5, final set. She misses her first serve in the net, and Holly edges inside her baseline. Live by the sword, die by the sword, I knew that come hell or high water Holly was going for it. A second serve is delivered to the Holly forehand and as she nails the return down the line for a clean winner, half the crowd is up on their feet in early celebration. Holly's familiar fist pump is out as she too assumes the ball is good, but a late cry of 'out' from the linesman says otherwise and the groan of the spectators gives away their disappointment. She could only have missed by a fraction (I'm sure I saw chalk fly up!) and it was a bitter, bitter blow.

With that miss, the momentum changed yet again in this gripping encounter and although Holly fought to the very end, perhaps with that missed match point so too disappeared a little self-belief, enough at least for Seone to wrap the match up 8-6 in the third set.

A brutal match to lose as a player. A brutal match for Holly to lose as her coach. But goodness me was I proud of her performance. Proud that she put herself on the line, proud that she played that return with such courageous purpose, proud that she represented herself so darn well and failed while daring greatly, never to be with those cold souls who know neither victory nor defeat. Good on ya, Hols!

Get out there, test where you're at, put yourself on the line. That's where the greatest learning is found, about yourself, others and this thing we call life!

CHAPTER 18

CHOOSE YOUR TOOLS WELL

I think it was 1997, although the date is irrelevant other than I was in my late 20s working as the Buckinghamshire County Performance Officer part-time, whilst continuing my Head Club Coach role at Halton.

Early spring and the promise of a busy summer on the courts, but still relatively quiet. I was sitting alone by the fire in the clubhouse with a mug of hot chocolate trying to rid myself of the cold that sets into your bones after a winter of braving the elements and an indoor dome that could have passed a health and safety inspection for a fridge.

The front door swings open and in walks a mountain of a man with a shock of frizzy hair, a glint in his eye and the languid walk of an athlete. A little look of Roger Federer I noticed.

'Hi I'm Bob,' he introduced himself in a deep, thick accent.

'From Austria,' he added.

'My English not so good, but I play tennis.'

For some reason, we tennis players seem to get a fairly immediate grip on each other, and I knew instinctively that Bob could play. Without too much chat and fussing, we agreed to hit a few balls the next day.

'Dress warm Bob,' I said, 'the dome can be cold.'

It must have been late afternoon or early evening when we met up to play. My Austrian is non-existent (although to be fair my mum's Swiss-German influence helped a little) and Bob's English was limited so with Bob looking a little like a puffed-up Michelin man (he had *really* taken my advice to stay warm) we walked on court with very little conversation. I cracked open a new can of balls which seemed to please him:

'Huh huh huh – new balls. Sehr gut.'

We began to hit and yes, Bob could play. He had a beautiful forehand and the ball came out from the middle of his Head Prestige (of course) with a satisfying thud. It looked a little like a table tennis bat in his hand. His backhand was a mix of one and two hands, the consistency of the strokes giving away the countless hours he must have toiled with Thomas Muster on the clay courts of his native Austria – or at least this was what I was making up in my head as we traded those first few balls! His feet never seemed to move, but he was always rock solid and in position behind the ball. Contrast this to me and my 'try harder' driver, full of hustle and bustle, on my toes with busy little steps around the ball, doing my best to impress!

After 10 minutes or so from hitting baseline to baseline where I felt very much the inferior player, I took the opportunity on a short ball to move into the net to take some volleys and a little solace in my comfort zone. I knew my volley could stand up to even the greatest of scrutiny and my confidence grew as I absorbed and redirected his steadily increasing pace, those thuds now more resembling canon shots.

We continued on for a while longer tentatively getting the measure of each other, the odd apology exchanged across the net when a stroke went awry. I had retreated back to the baseline to test my groundstrokes once again against the man machine, until there was a pause Bob's end of the court, a slight shake of the head and a then a slow walk to the net as if summoning me to join him. I walked up and asked him if he was OK.

With a shake of the head and a frown of concentration as if he were trying to remember the right words, he said, 'Ah, it's my vegetables. They are hurting.' The confused look on my face must have told the story because immediately Bob realised his error and we both burst out into fits of uncontrollable laughter. 'Vegetables! I mean vertebra! I look up in dictionary before I come today. My, how you say, back is bad?!'

Poor Bob. He had been anticipating this and had looked up 'back' in the dictionary. Coming away with 'vertebra', under the pressure of the moment he came out with 'vegetables'.

It broke the ice and was in fact the beginning of what is a beautiful friendship. We quickly adopted Bob into our group, and it was an incredibly proud moment when I was invited to Austria do the reading at Bob and Michi's wedding in 2006.

You see, that's what sport does. It brings people together and nearly all of my closest friendships, going way back to being a 13-year-old in Tucson, Arizona, have at least had tennis as the starting point.

'Vegetables' was certainly not the only gaff Bob made over the years. His English is now impeccable and he has worked incredibly hard at it, but there were a few more classics. We met up one evening in the pub after a long day at work and Bob walked in a little late to join us, still in suit and tie although the knot was by now halfway down his chest and the top couple of buttons undone.

He explained that he had been driving up to Manchester that morning. The weather was horrible and he kept on coming across an overhead sign saying FO9. FO9 he thought to himself, what's that? So he rang his colleague driving in the car ahead to ask.

'Fog, you idiot Bob,' came the reply. Slightly more colourful language was actually applied here but certainly not fit for these pages!

Amongst all we got up to, my greatest moments with Bob were spent on court. In those days, he always carried three rackets with him: a pair of Head Prestiges but the third was a mysterious black version of what I presumed was the same but with no markings or print, and rarely if ever used. When quizzed about it, he just simply said, 'Ah, this is the man's racket.'

Say no more, Bob.

It was in the days of the National Club League (NCL) and Halton were playing a match down towards the south coast, against Winchester Tennis Club if my memory serves me correctly. It was an incredibly tight match and we had entered the famous tiebreak shoot-out after being all square after regulation time. Bob and I were to play the doubles rubber of the shoot-out. It was fair to say that Bob hadn't been having the greatest day on court, had lost his singles and hadn't contributed much to our doubles either, but just before we walked on to play he said, 'Now, time for the man's racket!' and he pulled the mysterious weapon out of his bag. 'But Bob,' I said, 'you never use it. Surely now isn't the time. C'mon man, no messing around. We need this!'

The tiebreak began and I can honestly tell you, that against some really strong opposition, any ball Bob touched he hit for a clean winner and we ripped through it to win with ease.

'There you go, you see, the man's racket,' he concluded as we shook hands at the end.

Choose your racket well!

C H A P T E R   1 9

CAN YOU TEACH IT?

2015 was a remarkable year for Serena Williams with her amazing run for a calendar year Grand Slam ending in the semi-finals of the US Open in perhaps one of the biggest upsets ever as Roberta Vinci took the deciding set 6-4 to seal victory and set up a fairytale all-Italian final with her great friend and Federation Cup team-mate Flavia Pennetta.

Serena's calendar year Grand Slam run (when all four majors are won in the same year; the last player to do this was Steffi Graf in 1988) began with a 6-3, 7-6 victory over Maria Sharapova in January. It continued in late spring at the French Open where she beat Lucie Safarova 6-3, 6-7, 6-2 in what was her fifth three-set victory of the tournament. Twenty-four hours before the final, Serena was so ill with flu that she considered pulling out, but declaring herself fit enough to compete enabled her to close within two titles of Steffi's Open era record of 22 Grand Slam singles titles. Another amazing run at Wimbledon saw her arrive at the US Open in September on the cusp of achieving what very few players have done in the history of the sport. It really was a case of the only person being able to beat Serena was Serena, and this turned out to be the case as she put in a performance full of anxiety and nerves which allowed Vinci, playing some great tennis it must be said, to make the most of the opportunity afforded.

But history aside, let's just roll back to the final at Roland Garros against Safarova. Serena had just hit a blazing forehand return winner to go up 3-1 in the first set, and commentator Chris Evert said, 'You can't teach that – timing, balance, anticipation.' Well, having some deeply held values around learning, skill acquisition and of course the integrity of my profession, I quickly declared that this was one of the most ridiculous comments so far during this French Open.

Of course you can teach timing, balance, and anticipation but I guess what Chris Evert was really referring to is the great nature versus nurture debate raging on through sport and education at the moment as well as being explored by several authors mentioned in this book including Dr Carol Dweck and Daniel Coyle, and including others such as Matthew Syed, Malcolm Gladwell, and Josh Waitzkin to name but a few.

To further my own learning in this area, I recently read a fascinating book by David Epstein called *The Sports Gene – Talent, practice and the truth about success.*

I love his opening paragraph:

Micheno Lawrence was a sprinter on my high school track team. The son of Jamaican parents, he was short and doughy and his bulging paunch poked at the holes of his marina, the mesh top that some Jamaicans on the team wore to practice. He worked at McDonald's after school, and team-mates joked that he partook too often in the product. But it didn't stop him from being head-whipping fast.

Epstein goes on to introduce the nature versus nurture debate with this:

The broad truth is that nature and nurture are so interlaced in any realm of athletic performance that the answer is always: it's both. But that is not a satisfactory endpoint in science. Scientists must ask, "How, specifically, might nature and nurture be at work here?" and "How much does each contribute?" In pursuit of answers to these questions, sports scientists have trundled into the era of modern genetic research. This book is my attempt to trace where they have gone and to examine much of what is known or haggled over about the innate gifts of elite athletes.

So what of Serena's timing, balance and anticipation? How much of her talent in this area is gifted and how much is learned through the hours of deep practice and exposure to the game? And for that matter, what does it mean to the coach, the parent who is bringing up kids in sport, and indeed for the kids themselves? Well, I'll leave you to explore Epstein's work in more detail, but I do have a few anecdotes and thoughts to share on the subject.

I remember the first time being introduced to a six-year-old boy called Robert Mariconda by his then coach Hilary Evans who had done an amazing job getting Rob and many others to fall in love with tennis.

'I've got a little player you should really see, Mike,' Hilary had said to me one day, so we arranged a time for Rob to come over with his dad to Halton. I remember him being quite small for his age, quiet and somewhat shy, though polite and confident enough to look me in the eye with an excited glint of expectation for the session to come. We began to rally back and forth, and what was immediately noticeable was his speed and desire to chase everything, but it was not until I went down his end to hand feed a few balls that I really noticed his eyes. As soon as I picked a ball out of the basket he immediately locked on to it, well before I was ready to throw it to him. He was, in fact, like a Labrador puppy less the bouncing excitement, eyes never leaving the ball, rapturously fixed upon it. The two things that stood out then were speed and eyes, and the eyes giving way to a particular mindset, attitude or ability to focus. I had a genuine sense as the coach that he had a particular genetic starting point in these two areas, the physical and the mental, and it would be a case of how practice and exposure to the game would develop these attributes. With this, he was also clearly falling in love with the game.

Other examples from my own experience come to mind. Katy Dunne as an 11-year-old had an uncanny ability to use her hands to disguise and change the direction of the ball at the last minute. Amanda Carreras, now ranked WTA 350, at a similar age had an apparent gift to generate amazing pace with very little perceived effort. Andy Murray, whom I coached for a few months in a squad at Sterling University in 1999 and who played on many occasions against one of my own pupils Mathew Brown, had an uncanny ability to unlock and then dismantle his opponent's game. Nature or nurture? Or both?

My own position is that we do indeed 'arrive' with a certain genetic (natural) starting point and with the same amount of quality practice and exposure to a sport, not everyone will get to the same level, unlike the now well-known 10,000-hour rule might imply. By the way, Epstein stresses it was never called a 'rule' by K. Anders Ericsson in his paper 'The Role of Deliberate Practice in the Acquisition of Expert Performance' and it frustrates me when advocates of early specialisation in sport use this argument to win business for their programmes. I also maintain these different genetic starting points can be both physical and mental and even the ability to practice may have genetic influences.

But practice of course, makes what? Yes, permanent! Not perfect, so be careful what you practice! And I'm a great believer in practice and that with real persistence over time kids can indeed develop a high skill level and, at the very least, become the very best they can be, within their own genetic framework. There is also a very strong link here to passion, and my understanding that passion for a sport does not come as some lightning bolt out of the sky, but from a position of where a child is introduced to a game, struggles and wrestles with it and in persistently doing so, develops a love and passion for it.

As parents and coaches therefore, it's so important to be aware what our kids are attracted to and what they in turn become passionate about, as before we begin any discussion on talent, ability, deep practice and the like, a love and passion for what you do must come first.

Look at Federer now at almost 35 years old and Serena at 33. Above and beyond all their gifts and talent, whether natural or nurtured, they love the sport, they love competing, they love the journey of continuous and never-ending improvement.

To support this we have posted the following quote attributed to Roger Federer on an outside wall leading to the courts at Halton:

Sometimes you're just happy playing. Some people, some media, unfortunately, don't understand that it's okay just to play tennis and enjoy it. They always think you have to win everything, it always needs to be a success story, and it's not, obviously, what is the point? Maybe you have to go back and think why have I started playing tennis? Because I just like it. It's actually sort of a dream hobby that became somewhat of a job. Some people just don't get that, ever.

Everyball, everyday, for everybody. Come on and join us!

CHAPTER 20

KEEP YOUR EYE ON THE BALL, SON

Balls have been a central theme running through this book, *everyball* taking on somewhat of a plurality in its meaning. Fighting for *everyball* implies doing it again and again and that means having a lot of balls, both literally and, dare I say it, figuratively. In this way, balls cost and the subject is always on the agenda.

A few years ago, I blogged that *balls* had been the prevailing topic of the week:

We tried the Babolat VS ball this morning in training. Not bad. We had a major clear-out of the ball shed – we can never keep it tidy – in doing this we had a good ball sort. Some made the cut to live another day, the rest consigned to the guide-dog collection. Phil, just about to head out on court for a lesson, had apparently lost his balls and asked me if I knew where they were. I thought the answer was obvious. Younger son Jude (7 years) has been pestering me all week for a new football, only because he and his brother have kicked all of theirs into the neighbour's garden and neighbour is not returning them. Possibly something about them hitting his roof on a fairly regular basis. Older son Joel (9 years) has decided to write a letter to him. It reads: 'Sorry for hitting your house, please forgive us. We will try not to hit them over. From Joel. P.S. – give our balls back.

My fellow tennis coaches across Great Britain would identify with the ball dilemma but also, I suspect, agree with me on my next point.

I'm pretty much always (yes, that's an absolute but it is qualified by a 'pretty much') asked two main questions at a dinner party once I've introduced myself and said what I do for a living.

Is that your full-time job?

What's wrong with British tennis?

Or variations of, such as: What would you do if you were in charge?

Well I have been heavily involved in British tennis since arriving in England in the summer of 1992 and beginning my full-time coaching career in early 1993 as a 23-year-old. That's 24 years at the coalface of the sport in this country. During that time I have been contracted out to work for the governing body (LTA) in various roles and have witnessed five or six regime changes at the top of the sport. It's hard to argue against the fact that during this time we have underperformed with the resources available to us. However, I'm always wary of pointing the finger because when you do, there are always three pointing right back at you. Just try it!

And perhaps like all of these things, it will be down to a host of factors, but here's my dinner party answers to the questions above:

Yes, it's my full-time job, and although I could probably list a host of things wrong with British tennis and what I would do if I were in charge, I prefer to focus on what's right about our sport in this country and indeed worldwide, and what it has personally given me and what I hope I have given back to it in return.

I have met and worked with some amazing people, many of whom I count as dear friends. I'd like to make special mention of my team of coaches at *Everyball Tennis*, both past and present, and the unstinting support you have given me over the years. What we've achieved so far in educating, motivating and inspiring through the power of our sport to help others become the best they can be could not have been done without you, and I look forward to the many more chapters yet to come.

I have coached some wonderful people, young and old, and it has been a privilege to do so. You know who you are and those singled out in this book have only been done so to help me illustrate a particular point, though I must thank you for your permission in allowing me to do so.

I think back to my introduction into coaching through three of my earliest mentors at the Tucson Racquet Club – Sam Cuilla, Mike Morse and Gary Engelbrecht – and soon after at the University of Arizona, Coach Wright and Coach Hagedorn. Body-surfing the north shore in Hawaii with you and the team Hagi following a tournament there is a memory I'll treasure forever and still have the photos to testify!

But most of all this crazy sport of tennis that has obsessed me for a lifetime comes down to my relationship with *everyball*. My early years growing up were punctuated by frequent goodbyes. I went to boarding school in Kenya as a seven-year-old and at 17 my parents and brother left Arizona to return to Europe leaving me to fly solo at university. Even when I eventually followed on five or so years later, Mum and Dad set out on a new adventure to France so times together as a family were generally short and sweet. We developed a fairly consistent and stoic goodbye routine, my father's parting advice always the same, 'Mike, keep your eye on the ball, son.'

What he meant by this of course was to stay focused on the right stuff, make the best decisions possible and stay clear of dark alleys! In short, watch the ball carefully and everything else will take care of itself. I guess that's where the seed of *Everyball* was really planted, and I hope you have enjoyed this book and have taken a few snippets here and there as you play the wider game of life. I wish you all the very best in this.

In closing, I'd like to mention my wonderful wife Suzie and my amazing boys Joel and Jude. Suzie has been a source of constant support and encouragement in both the writing of this book and also a patient rock through the many late nights and long weekends I have been at work over the years. Joel and Jude, I quite understand your confusion when as little boys you used to say, 'Daddy, why are you going out to play with the other children?' Although you both play tennis from time to time, it's wonderful to watch your relationship with *everyball* develop in other sports, football and cricket in particular, and I will take this opportunity of passing on my own father's advice.

'Keep your eye on the ball, son.'

Everyball that is.

REFERENCES

Introduction and back cover

Agassi, Andre, *Open An Autobiography.* London: HarperCollins Publishers, 2010

Chapter 7

Wooden, John; Jamieson, Steve, *Wooden.* Illinois: Contemporary Publishing Company, 1997

Chapter 9

Frankl, Viktor, *Man's Search For Meaning.* Rider, 2004

Chapter 13

Grylls, Bear, *A Survival Guide For Life.* Bantam Press, 2012

Chapter 14

Pink, Dan, TED talk titled 'The Puzzle of Motivation' (filmed in 2009 at TEDGlobal 2009)

Chapter 15

Godin, S. 'Laziness.' sethgodin.typepad.com/seths_blog/2010/11/laziness.html. November 04 2010

Nadal, Rafael with Carlin, John, *Rafa My Story.* Sphere, 2011

Coyle, Daniel, *The Talent Code.* New York: Bantam, 2009

Chapter 19

Epstein, David, *The Sports Gene.* London: Yellow Jersey Press, 2014

ABOUT THE AUTHOR
MICHAEL JAMES

*This picture was taken by coach and colleague
Javier Gutiérrez Polo, or simply 'Guti' as we know him!*

Mike was born on 11 August 1968 in Nairobi, Kenya to a Swiss mother and English father. Attending boarding school at Kenton College from seven years old he quickly became sport obsessed, was a Kenyan junior national champion in the pool, and played football, rugby, hockey, cricket and tennis in equal measure. In all these sports, his elder brother Steven was his greatest tutor, and his first victory over him on a tennis court built in the Langata garden by his father remains a clear memory (to both brothers – there is a chapter dedicated to this in the book!) and ignited Mike's love affair with the sport.

Mike's love for tennis was further fuelled on the hard courts of Tucson, Arizona where the family moved in 1982. There, Mike played high school and then Division 1 college tennis for the University of Arizona Wildcats whilst studying for his BA in History and English.

In 1993 Mike moved to England to pursue a career in coaching and the last 20 years or more have seen him work extensively across British tennis as County Performance Officer for Buckinghamshire and Hertfordshire, National Performance Officer for Scotland (he counts himself lucky enough to have spent a little time with Andy and Jamie Murray as youngsters), travel extensively across Europe and work with a number of top nationally and internationally ranked junior and senior players.

He is currently Director of Tennis for Halton UK, one of the leading tennis clubs in Great Britain, and is founder of its much admired coaching brand, *Everyball Tennis* which services three clubs and over 20 outreach centres across the local community. Mike is an LTA Level 5 Master Performance Coach, and an LTA Coach Education tutor and consultant.

A fascination with personal and organisational change and development, high performance teamwork, and developing the mindset for success has led Mike to explore the work of the performance coach across other sports as well as into business and education.

He has recently founded a new branch of Halton UK called CHILDS (The Chiltern Institute of Learning, Development and Sport), with the objective of helping individuals, teams and organisations *win*. CHILDS defines winning as 'identifying, mobilising and gathering all our resources to go as far as we can', which ultimately sums up Mike's mission to help others grow, develop and thrive in whatever walk of life they find themselves in.

Mike is happily married to Suzie with two boys, Joel (13) and Jude (11), and lives in Berkhamsted, Hertfordshire.

9 781784 520861